Emocje

Emotions

Did you know that a baby's colour vision isn't fully developed until around 5 months old? Red is one of the first colours your baby will see, but until then, they can only see **black, white and grey** tones in a blurry world around them.

WHAT ARE THE BENEFITS OF HIGH CONTRAST BOOKS FOR YOUR BABY?

- **VISUAL DEVELOPMENT**
- **COGNITIVE DEVELOPMENT**
- **SOCIAL DEVELOPMENT**

This book is not only a chance to bond with your little one, but the black and white shapes that fill the pages will teach them all about the world around them.

Szczęśliwy

Happy

Smutny

Sad

Przestraszony

Afraid

Zdziwiony

Surprised

Zakochany

In love

Rozczarowany

Disappointed

Spokojny

Calm

Zrzędliwy

Grumpy

Dowcipny

Funny

Zmieszany

Confused

Zmartwiony

Worried

Zadowolony

Content

Radosny

Joyful

Zakłopotany

Embarrassed

Zmęczony

Tired

Zdenerwowany

Upset

THANK YOU
FOR YOUR PURCHASE

TO GET MORE
FREEBIES
SIGN UP HERE

HTTPS://AGNIESZKACIACH.COM
/SPTHANKYOU

Tip For Parents

This Book You Can Reuse Once Your Child is Older!
Just Cut Out The Figures and Lablels...